Iris Apfel

A Tapestry of Style, Creativity, and Unapologetic Individuality

By

Neil Potter

About the author

Neil Potter, an avid admirer of the intersection between art and personal expression, delves into the vibrant life of Iris Apfel in "Iris Apfel: A Tapestry of Style, Creativity, and Unapologetic Individuality." As a passionate storyteller and connoisseur of the extraordinary, Neil brings a keen eye for detail and a deep appreciation for the transformative power of self-expression to this exploration of Apfel's life.

Drawing inspiration from the boundless creativity and resilience embodied by Iris Apfel, Neil Potter weaves together a narrative that transcends the realms of fashion and design. With a background in capturing the essence of remarkable lives, Neil is dedicated to unraveling the layers of Iris Apfel's legacy, inviting readers on a captivating journey through the tapestry of a truly exceptional existence.

"Iris Apfel" is not just a biography; it is a tribute to the indomitable spirit of a woman who defied conventions, celebrated diversity, and left an indelible mark on the canvas of style. Neil's passion for storytelling is evident in his meticulous exploration of Apfel's life, providing readers with a front-row seat to the captivating story of a fashion icon whose legacy continues to inspire and resonate across generations.

Appreciation

Dear Reader,

Thank you for welcoming "Iris Apfel: A Tapestry of Style, Creativity, and Unapologetic Individuality" into your collection. Your choice to explore the vibrant life of Iris Apfel is a celebration of a remarkable journey—a journey marked by creativity, resilience, and an unwavering commitment to embracing one's unique identity.

As you delve into the pages of this book, I invite you to join me on a captivating exploration of Iris Apfel's extraordinary life. Her story is more than a biography; it's an odyssey through the realms of fashion, art, and the transformative power of self-expression. Together, we'll unravel the layers of Iris's legacy, discovering the profound impact she has left on the world of style.

I hope this book serves as a source of inspiration, encouraging you to embrace your individuality and celebrate the beauty found in authenticity. Thank you for embarking on this journey with me. May the pages of "Iris Apfel" weave a tapestry of inspiration and leave an indelible mark on your own appreciation for creativity and personal style.

Warm regards,

Neil Potter

Copyright

Dedication

This book is dedicated to those who understand the artistry of life, appreciating the beauty found in embracing one's individuality. To the dreamers, the creators, and the unapologetic souls who color outside the lines, may "Iris Apfel: A Tapestry of Style, Creativity, and Unapologetic Individuality" be a tribute to your spirit.

In honoring the legacy of Iris Apfel, we celebrate not only her remarkable journey but also the collective journey of those who refuse to conform to societal expectations. This dedication extends to the free spirits who see fashion as a canvas for self-expression, the adventurers who believe in the transformative power of personal style, and the believers who recognize that true elegance lies in authenticity.

May the pages of this book resonate with your own pursuit of creativity and inspire you to weave a tapestry of life that reflects

Iris Apfel

the unique hues of your spirit. Thank you
for being a part of this vibrant journey.

— *Neil Potter*

Iris Apfel

Table of contents

Iris Apfel

Iris Apfel

Iris Apfel

Lessons learned and wisdom shared

Chapter Eight: Conclusion

Summarizing Iris Apfel's enduring legacy

Final thoughts on her extraordinary life

Introduction

In the captivating pages of this biography, we delve into the extraordinary life of Iris Apfel, a trailblazing force in the world of fashion and design. From her humble beginnings to the pinnacle of global recognition, Apfel's journey is a testament to her indomitable spirit and unparalleled sense of style. As we unravel the layers of her life, we discover the influences that shaped her, the milestones that defined her career, and the profound impact she has left on the fashion landscape. Join me on this exploration of Iris Apfel's life—a tapestry woven with passion, creativity, and an unwavering commitment to individuality.

Brief overview of Iris Apfel's impact

Iris Apfel's impact is nothing short of revolutionary in the realm of fashion and design. Renowned for her eclectic and bold style, she has redefined the concept of beauty and challenged conventional norms. Apfel's influence extends beyond clothing, encompassing interior design and accessories. Through her fearless approach to self-expression, she has become an icon, inspiring generations to embrace their uniqueness. With an unmatched flair for combining disparate elements, Iris Apfel has not only left an indelible mark on the fashion industry but has also become a symbol of embracing one's authentic self.

Setting the stage for her remarkable life

Amidst the backdrop of an evolving world, Iris Apfel emerged as a beacon of individuality and creativity. Born in 1921, her early years were witness to a changing society, and this dynamic environment laid the foundation for her distinctive approach to life and style. As the world navigated through cultural shifts and evolving norms, Iris embarked on a journey that would weave her into the fabric of fashion history. The stage was set for an extraordinary life—one marked by innovation, resilience, and an unapologetic celebration of uniqueness.

Chapter One: Early Life and Influences

Iris Apfel's journey began in Astoria, Queens, in 1921. Growing up in a diverse and vibrant neighborhood, her early years were shaped by a multicultural environment that would later influence her eclectic taste. From a young age, Apfel showed an interest in art and design, foreshadowing her future contributions to the world of fashion. As she navigated the challenges of the Great Depression, her resourcefulness and passion for creativity became apparent, laying the groundwork for the indomitable spirit that would characterize her approach to both life and style.

Childhood and upbringing

Iris Apfel spent her formative years in Queens, New York, in a close-knit family that valued individuality and self-expression. Raised by parents who encouraged her curiosity, she developed a keen eye for aesthetics early on. Apfel's childhood was shaped by the rich cultural tapestry of her neighborhood, fostering a sense of openness to diverse influences. The seeds of her later unconventional style were planted during these foundational years, where creativity and a love for exploration were nurtured within the framework of a supportive family environment.

Early interests in fashion and design

In her youth, Iris Apfel exhibited a burgeoning passion for fashion and design that set her apart. Fascinated by the world of textiles, colors, and patterns, she began cultivating her unique aesthetic sensibility. Apfel's early interest in fashion extended beyond trends; she explored thrift stores, seeking hidden treasures and honing her ability to curate distinctive ensembles. This early fascination with the artistry of clothing laid the groundwork for her future as a style icon, reflecting the seeds of creativity that would blossom into a remarkable career in the world of design.

Formative experiences shaping her unique style

Iris Apfel's unique style was shaped by a tapestry of formative experiences that enriched her perspective. From exploring European cultures during travels to immersing herself in the vibrant New York art scene, Apfel absorbed diverse influences that fueled her distinctive aesthetic. Her involvement in textile restoration projects and work with renowned designers provided a hands-on education, fostering an appreciation for craftsmanship and the beauty of the unconventional. These formative experiences not only refined her eye for design but also contributed to the kaleidoscopic tapestry of influences that define Iris Apfel's inimitable and enduring style.

Chapter Two: Career Beginnings

Embarking on her career journey, Iris Apfel's early foray into the fashion industry was marked by a blend of passion and innovation. As an interior designer, she and her husband, Carl Apfel, established the textile firm Old World Weavers. This venture not only showcased her flair for design but also laid the foundation for her future impact. Apfel's unique approach to combining disparate elements caught the attention of influential figures, propelling her into the realm of high fashion collaborations and transforming her into a sought-after tastemaker. The genesis of her illustrious career was characterized by a fearless pursuit of creativity and a willingness to challenge conventional norms.

Entry into the fashion industry

Iris Apfel's entry into the fashion industry was marked by a bold and distinctive approach. Despite not conforming to traditional standards of beauty, her unique style captured the attention of the fashion elite. Apfel's groundbreaking work as an interior designer and her penchant for incorporating vintage and ethnic pieces into her wardrobe set her apart. This non-traditional entry into the fashion scene positioned her as a captivating and influential figure, ultimately paving the way for her iconic status as a fashion icon and entrepreneur.

Notable collaborations and projects

Iris Apfel's career is adorned with notable collaborations and projects that have left an indelible mark on the fashion landscape. Her groundbreaking work with the Metropolitan Museum of Art on the Costume Institute's "Rara Avis" exhibition solidified her reputation as a style maven. Collaborations with renowned brands like MAC Cosmetics and HSN showcased her diverse influence, while her role as a muse for designers such as Ralph Rucci added a layer of sophistication to her legacy. Apfel's ability to seamlessly blend her eclectic style with mainstream projects has made her a sought-after collaborator, leaving an enduring imprint on the intersection of art, fashion, and design.

Establishing her distinctive brand

Iris Apfel's journey in establishing her distinctive brand was a testament to her unparalleled vision and entrepreneurial spirit. With her vibrant personality and eclectic style at the forefront, Apfel launched her own line of accessories, including jewelry and eyewear. This venture not only showcased her artistic sensibilities but also reinforced her belief in the power of individuality. The Iris Apfel brand became synonymous with embracing uniqueness and celebrating the beauty of unconventional style, resonating with a diverse audience and solidifying her status as an icon in the world of fashion and design.

Chapter Three: The Rise of Iris Apfel

The rise of Iris Apfel is a narrative marked by a meteoric ascent from an unconventional figure to a revered icon in the world of fashion and design. As her eclectic style and fearless approach gained widespread recognition, Apfel became a symbol of individuality and self-expression. Her inclusion in high-profile fashion events, collaborations with esteemed designers, and the release of documentaries showcasing her life elevated her to legendary status. The fashion industry and beyond came to embrace the "Iris Apfel aesthetic," turning her into a cultural phenomenon and reaffirming that true style knows no boundaries.

Recognition and fame

Iris Apfel's journey to recognition and fame is a tale of authenticity resonating with a global audience. Her unapologetic embrace of personal style garnered attention, leading to features in prominent fashion publications. Apfel's distinct presence at high-profile events and collaborations catapulted her into the public eye, earning her a dedicated following. As a cultural icon, she received accolades, awards, and even became the subject of documentaries, solidifying her status as a revered figure in the realms of fashion and design. Iris Apfel's recognition and fame are not just about style but a celebration of the extraordinary impact one individual can have on shaping the conversation around beauty and individuality.

Iconic moments in her career

Iris Apfel's career is studded with iconic moments that have etched her name into the annals of fashion history. From being the first living person to have an exhibition at the Metropolitan Museum of Art's Costume Institute to her role as a muse for renowned designers like Albert Kriemler, each moment underscored her transformative influence. The release of the documentary "Iris" further immortalized her unique journey, captivating audiences worldwide. Apfel's appearances on prestigious stages, including fashion weeks and TED Talks, stand as timeless milestones, contributing to her status as an enduring icon in the ever-evolving tapestry of style and creativity.

Pioneering contributions to the fashion world

Iris Apfel's pioneering contributions to the fashion world are nothing short of revolutionary. Her fearless rejection of societal norms redefined beauty standards and inspired a paradigm shift in the industry. Apfel's advocacy for age inclusivity in fashion challenged stereotypes, while her collaborations brought a fresh perspective to renowned brands. As a style influencer, she championed the idea that true fashion is an art form accessible to all. Through her bold choices and distinctive approach, Iris Apfel has left an indelible imprint, not just as a fashion icon, but as a trailblazer whose influence continues to shape the evolving landscape of the fashion world.

Chapter Four: Personal Life

In her personal life, Iris Apfel navigated a rich tapestry of relationships and experiences. Her enduring partnership with husband Carl Apfel was not only a love story but also a collaborative journey in business and design. Together, they traveled the world, collecting unique pieces that would later become integral to Iris's iconic style. Apfel's personal life reflects a harmonious blend of creativity, companionship, and a shared passion for exploration, offering a glimpse into the human behind the fashion legend.

Relationships and family

Iris Apfel's relationships and family played a pivotal role in shaping the fabric of her life. Her enduring marriage to Carl Apfel was not only a romantic partnership but also a dynamic collaboration in business and design. The Apfels shared a love for travel and exploration, creating a bond woven with shared experiences and a mutual appreciation for art and style. While Iris and Carl didn't have children of their own, their family extended to friends, collaborators, and a global community captivated by the Apfels' unique charm and creativity. The interconnected threads of relationships and family underscored the warmth and vibrancy that defined Iris Apfel's personal life.

Balancing personal and professional spheres

Iris Apfel masterfully navigated the delicate balance between her personal and professional spheres. While her professional life was marked by high-profile collaborations and global recognition, Apfel maintained a strong sense of authenticity and connection to her personal values. Her enduring partnership with Carl Apfel showcased a seamless integration of personal and professional collaboration, adding depth to both aspects of her life. Apfel's ability to weave her personal experiences, relationships, and adventures into her professional journey stands as a testament to her holistic approach, demonstrating that a life well-lived encompasses the harmonious interplay of personal and professional realms.

Chapter Five: Challenges and Triumphs

Iris Apfel's life journey is woven with both challenges and triumphs, creating a rich tapestry of resilience and accomplishment. From overcoming societal norms that often favored conventional beauty standards to navigating the complexities of the fashion industry, Apfel faced challenges with unwavering determination. Her triumphs, on the other hand, are reflected in her trailblazing impact on style, her iconic collaborations, and the global recognition she garnered. The juxtaposition of challenges and triumphs in Apfel's life adds depth to her narrative, portraying a woman who not only confronted adversity but also emerged victorious, leaving an indelible mark on the world of fashion and design.

Obstacles faced along the way

Iris Apfel encountered various obstacles on her remarkable journey. In an industry often fixated on youth and conformity, Apfel faced resistance to her unconventional style and age-defying approach. Overcoming stereotypes and societal expectations, she carved a niche for herself, challenging the notion that fashion is exclusive to a particular age or aesthetic. Apfel's resilience in navigating these obstacles not only solidified her status as a fashion icon but also paved the way for a more inclusive and diverse representation within the industry. Her ability to turn challenges into opportunities reflects the enduring spirit that defines her extraordinary life.

Resilience and perseverance

Iris Apfel's life story is a testament to resilience and perseverance. In the face of societal expectations and industry norms, she embraced her unique style with unyielding confidence. Apfel's resilience shone through during moments of adversity, reinforcing her belief in the power of individuality. Her ability to persevere, whether in challenging the status quo or navigating the complexities of the fashion world, became a guiding force in her journey. Iris Apfel's unwavering commitment to staying true to herself, coupled with her persistent pursuit of creativity, showcases a remarkable resilience that has left an enduring impact on the realms of fashion and design.

Major achievements and milestones

Iris Apfel's life is adorned with major achievements and milestones that have left an indelible mark on the world of fashion and design. Some of these significant moments include:

- **Metropolitan Museum of Art Exhibition:**

Being the first living person to have a solo exhibition at the Metropolitan Museum of Art's Costume Institute, titled "Rara Avis."

- **Documentary "Iris":**

The release of the documentary "Iris" in 2014, directed by Albert Maysles, which provided an intimate and insightful look into her life and career.

- **Collaborations with Designers:**

Serving as a muse and collaborator for esteemed designers like Albert Kriemler and creating her own line of accessories.

- **Global Recognition:**

Receiving numerous accolades and awards, cementing her status as a global fashion icon.

- **Advocacy for Age Inclusivity:**

Pioneering age inclusivity in fashion and challenging stereotypes associated with aging.

- **Entrepreneurial Ventures:**

Successfully establishing her own brand, including a line of accessories, and showcasing her unique style on a global stage.

These achievements and milestones collectively paint a portrait of Iris Apfel as a trailblazer, shaping the fashion landscape and inspiring generations with her creativity and individuality.

Chapter Six: Legacy

Iris Apfel's legacy is a vibrant tapestry woven with threads of creativity, individuality, and resilience. Her impact on the world of fashion and design transcends trends and seasons, leaving an enduring imprint on the industry. Apfel's legacy is characterized by:

- **Style Icon:**

Cementing her status as a timeless style icon, inspiring countless individuals to embrace their uniqueness and express themselves fearlessly.

- **Innovator and Visionary:**

Introducing a fresh perspective to fashion by blending disparate elements and challenging conventional norms, showcasing her innovation and visionary approach.

- **Advocate for Inclusivity:**

Pioneering age inclusivity in fashion, advocating for diversity, and encouraging individuals to celebrate their individual beauty regardless of societal expectations.

- **Entrepreneurial Spirit:**

Establishing her own brand and contributing to the entrepreneurial spirit in the fashion industry.

- **Cultural Phenomenon:**

Becoming a cultural phenomenon, celebrated not only for her eclectic style but also for her authenticity, wit, and wisdom.

Iris Apfel's legacy extends far beyond the confines of the fashion world, touching hearts and inspiring a global community to boldly embrace their unique identities. Her enduring influence continues to shape conversations about self-expression and creativity, leaving an indelible mark on the

Iris Apfel

evolving landscape of style and individuality.

Impact on fashion and design

Iris Apfel's impact on fashion and design is transformative, influencing the industry in profound ways:

- **Diversity and Inclusion:**

Apfel challenged traditional beauty standards, promoting diversity and inclusivity. Her presence emphasized that style knows no age, size, or conventional norms.

- **Eclectic Style:**

Renowned for her bold, eclectic style, Apfel inspired a shift towards embracing individuality in fashion. Her fearless combinations of patterns, textures, and accessories became a hallmark of her influence.

- **Ageless Elegance:**

As a nonagenarian style icon, Apfel shattered age-related stereotypes in the fashion world. Her ability to remain relevant and influential at any age has had a lasting impact on perceptions of beauty and style.

- **Entrepreneurial Inspiration:**

Establishing her own brand showcased the potential for personal expression in entrepreneurship. Apfel's ventures inspired a new generation to embrace their creativity in the business of fashion and design.

- **Museum Recognition:**

The Metropolitan Museum of Art's recognition with a solo exhibition underlines her significance in the fashion canon, solidifying her place as a living legend.

Iris Apfel's influence resonates as a force that transcends trends, emphasizing the enduring power of authenticity, creativity, and breaking boundaries in the ever-evolving world of fashion and design.

Continued influence and relevance

Iris Apfel's continued influence and relevance persist as a testament to the timeless nature of her impact:

- **Generational Inspiration:**

Apfel's legacy continues to inspire new generations, fostering a culture that celebrates individuality and creative expression.

- **Fashion as Art:**

Her unique approach to fashion, treating it as a form of art, has influenced contemporary designers and enthusiasts to view clothing as a canvas for personal expression.

- **Social Media and Digital Influence:**

In the age of social media, Apfel's iconic style remains a popular subject of admiration and emulation, showcasing her enduring relevance in digital spaces.

- **Inclusive Representation:**

Her advocacy for diversity and age inclusivity has resonated within an industry increasingly focused on representing a broader range of identities.

- **Collaborations and Partnerships:**

Ongoing collaborations with brands and designers demonstrate that Apfel's distinctive style continues to captivate and contribute to the evolution of fashion.

As a living legend, Iris Apfel's influence remains a dynamic force, shaping the way we perceive and engage with fashion, design, and the celebration of individuality. Her impact is not confined to a specific era but continues to evolve, leaving an indelible mark on the ever-changing landscape of style and culture.

Contributions to culture and style

Iris Apfel's contributions to culture and style are profound and multifaceted:

- **Cultural Icon:**

Apfel's vibrant personality and distinctive style have transformed her into a cultural icon, transcending the boundaries of the fashion world and resonating across diverse cultural spheres.

- **Style Philosophy:**

Her fearless approach to mixing patterns, textures, and accessories has become synonymous with an ethos of self-expression, inspiring individuals to break free from conventional fashion norms.

- **Documentary Impact:**

The documentary "Iris" provided a platform for Apfel's wit and wisdom, showcasing her life story and influencing how society perceives aging, fashion, and personal identity.

- **Educational Influence:**

Through her involvement in exhibitions and educational initiatives, Apfel has contributed to a broader understanding of fashion as an art form and a vehicle for self-discovery.

- **Global Influence:**

Apfel's global impact is evident in her collaborations with designers worldwide, making her a symbol of cross-cultural appreciation and inspiration.

By seamlessly blending her love for art, travel, and fashion, Iris Apfel has not only left an indelible mark on the world of style but has also enriched cultural conversations

Iris Apfel

around self-expression, diversity, and the enduring beauty of individuality.

Chapter Seven: Reflections

In reflecting on Iris Apfel's extraordinary life, one can't help but marvel at the tapestry she has woven. Her journey is a symphony of creativity, resilience, and authenticity—a melody that continues to resonate across the realms of fashion and design. Apfel's unwavering commitment to individuality, her fearless approach to style, and her ability to break down barriers in an industry often bound by conventions serve as an enduring source of inspiration. As we reflect on her legacy, we are reminded that true style is a reflection of one's inner spirit, and Iris Apfel has undeniably left an indelible imprint on the canvas of culture, encouraging us all to embrace the beauty of our unique selves.

Iris Apfel's perspective on her journey

Iris Apfel's perspective on her journey is a captivating blend of wisdom, humor, and authenticity. She views her life as a constant exploration of creativity and self-expression, emphasizing the importance of embracing individuality. Apfel often shares insights about the transformative power of personal style and the joy found in breaking fashion norms. Her reflections highlight the beauty in unconventional choices and the liberation that comes from being true to oneself. Apfel's journey, as seen through her lens, is a celebration of life as an ongoing adventure, an exploration of artistry, and a reminder that age is no barrier to living authentically and with unparalleled flair.

Lessons learned and wisdom shared

Iris Apfel's life imparts valuable lessons and profound wisdom:

- **Embrace Individuality:**

Apfel's mantra is to celebrate what makes you unique. She encourages people to express themselves authentically, irrespective of societal norms.

- **Style Knows No Age:**

Aging is not a limitation; it's an opportunity for continued self-expression. Apfel challenges the perception of age in the fashion industry and beyond.

- **Fearless Creativity:**

Apfel's fearless approach to combining patterns, textures, and accessories teaches us to embrace creativity without boundaries and to find beauty in unconventional choices.

- **Resilience Matters:**

Her resilience in the face of challenges illustrates the importance of perseverance and staying true to oneself, even in industries where conformity often prevails.

- **Life as an Adventure:**

Apfel sees life as an ongoing adventure, emphasizing the joy of discovery, whether in fashion, art, or personal growth.

In essence, Iris Apfel's lessons and wisdom inspire us to live with authenticity, creativity, and an unwavering commitment to self-expression. Her journey is a testament to the transformative power of embracing one's unique identity.

Chapter Eight: Conclusion

In conclusion, the life of Iris Apfel is a remarkable narrative of creativity, resilience, and unapologetic individuality. From her upbringing in Queens to becoming a global fashion icon, Apfel's journey transcends the confines of the industry, leaving an indelible mark on culture and style. Her fearless approach to fashion challenges norms and inspires generations to embrace their unique identities. Iris Apfel's enduring legacy is not merely about clothing; it's a celebration of the art of living authentically and with boundless creativity. As we reflect on her extraordinary life, we are reminded that true style is a reflection of the soul—an art form that Iris Apfel has mastered with unparalleled grace.

Summarizing Iris Apfel's enduring legacy

Iris Apfel's enduring legacy is a testament to her transformative influence on the fashion world and beyond. As a style icon, she shattered norms, celebrating individuality and diversity. Her fearless approach to fashion and design emphasized the timeless beauty of self-expression, inspiring generations to embrace uniqueness. Beyond clothing, Apfel's legacy is a beacon of resilience, encouraging us to navigate challenges with authenticity and creativity. Iris Apfel's impact extends far beyond trends; it's a profound cultural shift, leaving an indelible mark on the canvas of style, proving that true elegance lies in embracing one's authentic self.

Final thoughts on her extraordinary life

In reflecting on Iris Apfel's extraordinary life, one is struck by the vibrancy she brought to every aspect of her journey. Her story is a testament to the boundless possibilities of self-expression and the enduring power of individuality. Iris Apfel not only reshaped the landscape of fashion and design but also left an indelible mark on our collective understanding of beauty, creativity, and resilience. Her legacy is a celebration of a life lived authentically, fearlessly, and with an unwavering commitment to embracing the richness of every moment. Iris Apfel's extraordinary life will continue to inspire and resonate as a timeless reminder that true style is a reflection of the soul—a legacy that transcends trends and endures as a guiding light for generations to come.